**inside intelligence** presents

T0262500

The Scottish Premiere

# Tejas Verdes

**by Fermín Cabal**
**Translated by Robert Shaw**

# inside intelligence

# Tejas Verdes

by Fermín Cabal
Translated by Robert Shaw

*Cast*

| | |
|---|---|
| THE DISAPPEARED | |
| THE FRIEND | |
| THE DOCTOR | |
| THE GRAVEDIGGER | **MADELEINE POTTER** |
| THE INFORMER | |
| THE SPANISH LAWYER | |
| THE SOUL IN TORMENT | |

The performance lasts approximately 70 minutes.

There will be no interval.

| | |
|---|---|
| Director | **Robert Shaw** |
| Designer | **Sarah Paulley** |
| Lighting Designer | **Conleth White** |
| Stage Manager | **Catherine Lewis** |
| Assistant Director | **Alice Kornitzer** |
| Design Assistant | **Gillian Argo** |
| Producer | **Chris Foxon** |

First performance of this production as part of just
Festival at St John's, Princes Street, Edinburgh,
on 2 August 2013

This translation first produced at the Gate Theatre,
London, on 10 January 2005

**Madeleine Potter** | THE DISAPPEARED/ THE FRIEND/THE DOCTOR/THE GRAVEDIGGER/THE INFORMER/THE SPANISH LAWYER/THE SOUL IN TORMENT Madeleine's most notable film credits are with Merchant Ivory for whom she has done four films: *The Bostonians*, in which she starred with Vanessa Redgrave and Christopher Reeve (Best Actress with Vanessa Redgrave, International Film Festival, Delhi), *Slaves of New York*, *The Golden Bowl* and *The White Countess* (starring Ralph Fiennes) released in 2005. Other film credits include *Two Evil Eyes* directed by Dario Argento, *Bloodhounds of Broadway* directed by Howard Brookener, *The Chosyu Five* directed by Sho Igarishi and *Red Lights* directed by Roderigo Cortes.

Her London stage work includes the acclaimed *After Mrs Rochester* (People's Choice Best Actress Nominee) in which she starred with Diana Quick, and which won an *Evening Standard* Award and *Time Out* Best Play of the Year.

Also in the West End she starred with Macaulay Culkin and Irene Jacob in *Madame Melville*, *All My Sons* directed by Howard Davies and *Southwark Fair* directed by Nicholas Hytner, both for the Royal National Theatre, and *An Ideal Husband*, with Martin Shaw, directed by Sir Peter Hall.

Madeleine was in the first production of Sarah Kane's *4:48 Psychosis* with Daniel Evans and Jo McInnes at the Royal Court, directed by James MacDonald. Madeleine's most recent theatre credits include *Electra* directed by Carrie Cracknell at the Gate and Latitude Festival, *The Internationalist* directed by Natalie Abrahami, *Mother of Him* at the Courtyard by award-winning writer Evan Placey, *The Water's Edge* at the Arcola and *Broken Glass* with Anthony Sher at the Tricycle directed by Iqbal Khan.

She has also starred in numerous Broadway productions including *An Ideal Husband* directed by Sir Peter Hall, *The Master Builder* (opposite Lynn Redgrave), *The Crucible* (with Martin Sheen), *Getting Married*, Steven Berkoff's *Metamorphosis* (opposite Milhail Baryshnikov), David Hare's *Plenty* and *Slab Boys* (opposite Sean Penn, Val Kilmer and Kevin Bacon).

Other New York credits include Eliza Doolittle in *Pygmalion*, Pegeen in *Playboy of the Western World*, Nora in *The Plough and the Stars*, Lady Anne in *Richard III* (with Kevin Kline) and the premieres of *Lydie Breeze*, directed by Louis Malle, and Marion in *Abingdon Square*, written and directed by Irene Fornes. She played Ophelia in *Hamlet* for Lindsay Anderson at the Folger Shakespeare Theatre and Rosalind in *As You Like It* at the Williamstown Theatre Festival.

Madeleine can currently be seen playing resident Psychiatrist Sharon Kozinsky in BBC's *Holby City*. She has been heard in many radio plays for the BBC.

From time to time, Madeleine is a teacher in Oxford for the British American Drama Academy and has led workhops for Synergy Theatre Project and at HMP Brixton for the London Shakespeare Workout.

## Fermín Cabal | Playwright

Fermín Cabal, born in León in 1948, is one of the generation of Spanish theatre artists who formed the independent theatre movement following the end of the Fascist dictatorship in Spain in the mid-1970s.

In his early career he worked as an actor, director and playwright with such groups as Tábano, Los Goliardos and El Gayo Vallecano. By the end of the 1970s and into the 1980s he became recognised as one of Spain's important new voices in the theatre with his plays *Tú estás loco, Briones (You're Crazy, Briones)* (1978), *¿Fuiste a ver a la abuela? (Did You Go to See Grandmother?)* (1979), *¡Vade retro! (Get Thee Behind Me!)* (1982) and *Esta noche, gran velada (Big Do Tonight)* (1983).

In 1985 Cabal co-authored with José Luís Alonso de Santos *Teatro Español de los 80*, a collection of interviews with the leading theatre artists of their generation. His next play *Caballito del diablo (Dragonfly)* came out in the same year and in 1986 he wrote his first film-script, *La reina del mate (Checkmate Queen)*. From 1986 to 1988 he wrote the television series *Ramper*. In 1990 he returned to the stage with his play *Ello Dispara (¡shoot!)*. This was followed by *Entre tinieblas (Dark Habits)* (1992), a play based on Pedro Almodóvar's film of the same name, *Travesía (Crossing the Line)* (1993, winner of the Tirso de Molina and Teatro de Rojas prizes) and *Castillos en el aire (Castles in the Sky)* (1995).

Cabal has also translated and adapted several English and American plays for the Spanish stage, including David Mamet's *American Buffalo*, Christopher Durang's *Beyond Therapy*, Martin McDonagh's *The Beauty Queen of Leenane* and Terry Johnson's *Hysteria*.

Among his recent writing have been 24 episodes of the Spanish version of the American sitcom *Golden Girls* and his versions of *Electra* (1997, based on the play by Jean Giraudoux) and *Medea* (1998) both premiered in the Roman theatre at Mérida, for whom he has also written a version of the Agrippina story. In 2005, he directed his adaptation of *The Kitchen* by Arnold Wesker in Madrid. In the last two years he has published *Modern Spanish Playwriting (Dramaturgía Española Actual* – interviews with 24 contemporary

Spanish playwrights), a biography of Cardinal Tarancón, who headed the Catholic Church in Spain during the transition from dictatorship to democracy in the 1970s, and *Dakar-Madrid con Ricardo* – a journal of the well-known car rally.

His film *Ni piés ni cabeza*, about the Spanish police force known as the Guardia Civil, opened in 2012; November 2013 sees the opening of his latest play *Un mundo mejor ya está aquí (Brave New World is Here)*.

*Tejas Verdes* was commissioned by Aran Dramática, an exiled Chilean theatre company based in the Spanish city of Badajoz, where it premiered in 2002 before its Madrid debut in 2005.


**Robert Shaw** | Translator and Director

Robert graduated from Cambridge University. In May 1995 he founded Inside Intelligence.

Robert's translation of Fermín Cabal's *Tejas Verdes* received its UK premiere at the Gate in 2005 with Gemma Jones, directed by Thea Sharrock. It was first performed in a reading at Jermyn Street Theatre in 2002 directed by Robert with Joely Richardson and Patsy Byrne.

Theatre as director includes *Happy New* (Trafalgar Studios), the British premieres of *The Woods* (Finborough Theatre) and his own translations of *Ana in Love* (Hackney Empire) and *íshoot!* (Jermyn Street Theatre). Other theatre includes *One God, One Farinelli!* (BAC),*Three Women* (Jermyn Street Theatre, London, Assembly Rooms, Edinburgh and 59E59 Theatre, New York), his own adaptation of *Some Gorgeous Accident* (Assembly Rooms, Edinburgh), his own adaptation of *Up To Now* (Edinburgh Festival), *Teddy and Topsy* (Hill Street, Edinburgh and Old Red Lion Theatre, London), *Poem Without a Hero* (Edinburgh Festival), *As You Like It* (Cambridge, Jermyn Street Theatre and Greenwich Festival), *The Investigation* (Richmond), *Inferno XXXIII* (Gate Theatre), *Reunion* (Duke's Playhouse, Lancaster), *Tell Me That I'm Dreaming* (The Place), *Measure for Measure* (Chelsea Theatre), *The Poker Session* and *The Ruling Class* (Putney Arts Theatre), *A Little Night Music* (Cambridge), *The Hostage (An Giall)* (Edinburgh Festival), *Waiting for Lefty*, *Statements after an Arrest under the Immorality Act* and *Fear* (Sir Richard Steele Theatre, of which Robert was joint Artistic Director).

Theatre as assistant director includes Roger Michell's production of *Sexual Perversity in Chicago* (Sir Richard Steele Theatre) and Keith Hack's production of *The Dance of Death* starring Alan Bates and Frances de la Tour (Riverside Studios).

Opera includes*The Medium* and *The Lighthouse* (BAC), and *The Prince* and *Dutchman* (Riverside Studios).

Until recently Robert was the International Representative of the Chekhov Memorial Theatre in Taganrog, Chekhov's birthplace.

**Sarah Paulley** | Designer
Sarah Paulley started working as a designer at Oxford University where she was supposed to be reading History and went on to postgraduate training at the Motley Theatre Design Course. Throughout the 70s she worked for a range of alternative companies, including Avon Touring and 7:84 England and in 1978 became Head of Design at Theatre Royal Stratford East.
Thereafter she combined teaching with freelance design and production management, mainly for site-specific projects. Since 1990 she has lived in Glasgow, and worked in the Tron, the Arches, Tramway and for Bard in the Botanics as well as teaching at the Glasgow School of Art.
Currently she teaches at Queen Margaret University Edinburgh as Lecturer in Scenography and designs shows when she can, most recently *Allotment* and *Threads*, both Fringe First winners for Nutshell Productions.
She also runs the summer theatre design course Scenehouse Intro and has a prop and costume warehouse (Theatre Stuff Ltd.) in partnership with Joanna Kennedy.

**Conleth White** | Lighting Designer
Conleth has been designing lighting in Ireland for some years. Recent work includes *Carthaginians*, *Performances* and *Translations* (directed Adrian Dunbar, Millennium Forum, Derry), the set/lighting/imagery for the 36th (Ulster) Division Memorial committee presentation of *From the Shipyard to the Somme* in East Belfast, Edna O'Brien's *Country Girls* (Red Kettle), *Titanic (Scenes from the British Wreck Commissioner's Inquiry,1912)*, by Owen McCafferty, directed by Charlotte Westenra which opened the Mac in Belfast, *The Chronicles of Long Kesh* (Tron Theatre, Glasgow, and Tricycle Theatre, London) and *I Once Knew A Girl...* (Teya Sepinuck, Theatre of Witness, The Playhouse, Derry).
Recently for DLR Glasthule Opera, he has lit and designed imagery for *La Traviata, The Magic Flute, Weeping Flowers* and *The Marriage Of Figaro* in the Pavilion, Dun Laoire, Dublin.
For Axis-Ballymun he has designed lighting for six plays by Dermot Bolger: *From These Green Heights, The Townlands of Brazil* (also in Teatr Polksi, Wroclaw), *The Consequences of Lightning, Walking the Road* (also in Leper, Belgium), *The Parting Glass* and *Tea Chests and Dreams*.
Conleth has lit many plays of Belfast playwright Marie Jones, including *Weddings, Weeans and Wakes* (Lyric Belfast), *Blind Fiddler* (Assembly Rooms, Edinburgh), *A Night in November* (Trafalgar Studio One London), *Lay Up Your Ends* and *HRT* (Grand Opera House, Belfast).

Recent site-specific/installations include *Green Street* in the Green Street Court House (Percolate, Dublin Fringe 12), *This is What We Sang* in the Belfast Synagogue and *5 in 1* at the Limavady Workhouse (Kabosh). Other site-specific/installation work includes *Macbeth* in Crumlin Road Gaol, Belfast, *(Replay)* and *The Tempest* in Kilmainham Gaol, Dublin (Island), *Binlids*, a community theatre piece on five stages in West Belfast & Lower Manhattan (Pam Brighton, Dubbeljoint) and *Northern Star* by Stewart Parker in the First Presbyterian Church Belfast (Stephen Rea, Tinderbox/Field Day). He toured to Belgrade, Taiwan and Denmark with Big Telly's swimming-pool production of *The Little Mermaid*. He was involved in the lighting for the NVA Divali, Eid-al-Fitr and Christmas Festivals of Light in the Hidden Gardens, Tramway, Glasgow 2003. He has also lit quite a few fashion shows for the Glasgow School of Art in the Arches, the Fruit Market and the Tramway.
Conleth was involved in the campaigns in Dublin to release The Birmingham Six and Guilford Four. He teaches lighting in Inchicore CFE in Dublin.

**Catherine Lewis** | Stage Manager
Catherine Lewis graduated in 2011 from the RSAMD with a BA in Technical and Production Arts. Previous productions include *Peter Grimes on the Beach* and *Les Mamelles de Tiresias* for Aldeburgh Music, *Project Colony*, *4:48 Psychosis* and *Elephant Man* for Fourth Monkey Theatre Company and *Madama Butterfly* for Grange Park Opera.

**Alice Kornitzer** | Assistant Director
Alice trained at Queen Margaret University, Edinburgh and Bristol University.
Alice has worked with the Berliner Ensemble and toured Europe extensively. Theatre includes *Happy New* (Trafalgar Studios), *Peer Gynt* (Berliner Ensemble), *The Fever* (Theater Unterm Dach), *God of Carnage* (Landestheater Linz) and *Allotment* (Nutshell Theatre).

**Gillian Argo** | Design Assistant
Gillian Argo has just completed her fifth summer with Bard in the Botanics, this year designing *Othello* and *Much Ado About Nothing*. Other recent productions include stage design for *Snow White* at the Byre, adapting her set for *Hairy Maclary and Friends* for an Australian tour, scenic painting for short fim *In Extremis* and prop making for *Hickory and Dickory Dock*. Most recently she was involved in creating *The Embassy*.

**Chris Foxon** | Producer

Chris read English at Oxford University and trained at the Central School of Speech & Drama on an AHRC Scholarship.

Theatre as producer includes *Happy New* (Trafalgar Studios), *The Fear of Breathing* (Finborough Theatre, transferring to Tokyo in November 2013), *The Madness of George III* (Oxford Playhouse), *I Didn't Always Live Here* and *Vibrant 2012 – A Festival of Finborough Playwrights* (Finborough Theatre), *Pilgrims* (Etcetera Theatre), *Grave Expectations* (Compass Theatre, St Albans South Signal Box and South Hill Park) and *Old Vic New Voices 24-Hour Plays 2012* (The Old Vic).

Theatre as assistant producer includes *Mudlarks* (HighTide Festival Theatre, Theatre503 and Bush Theatre), *On The Threshing Floor* (Hampstead Theatre) and 'Endless Poem' for *Rio Occupation London* (HighTide Festival Theatre and BAC).

Chris is the producer of the award-winning Papatango Theatre Company and New Writing Prize, whose acclaimed productions include *Foxfinder* by Dawn King and *Pack* by Louise Monaghan. In 2013 Papatango will develop work with Bristol Old Vic and the Finborough Theatre.

Chris is an interviewer for The Old Vic's T.S. Eliot Commissions.

**Special Thanks to**
Robbie Coltrane, Judi Dench, Jeremy Irons, Kirsten Rausing, Mrs Margaret Guido's Charitable Trust and The Coutts Charitable Trust, whose generous sponsorship made this production possible.

# inside intelligence

Inside Intelligence was founded by Robert Shaw in May 1995. *Tejas Verdes* perfectly expresses our determination to introduce British audiences to great work that would otherwise be foreign and inaccessible; we aim to present the best in new theatre writing and contemporary music theatre from around the globe. The actor, writer and composer are at the centre of our work.

Our most recent productions are the west end premiere of *Happy New* by BAFTA-nominee Brendan Cowell at Trafalgar Studios, the world premiere of *Teddy and Topsy*, Robert's play based on the love letters of Isadora Duncan to Gordon Craig, the world premiere of Robert's adaptation of *Some Gorgeous Accident* by James Kennaway at the Assembly Rooms in Edinburgh, Robert's adaptation of *Up To Now*, the autobiography of his grandfather, the English composer Martin Shaw, and the first ever staging of Anna Akhmatova's *Poem Without a Hero*, translated by DM Thomas.

We have also recently produced the first revival of *Three Women* by Sylvia Plath, which featured music by Schnittke. This was produced in London and Edinburgh in 2009 and in New York at 59E59 Theaters in October 2010 to critical acclaim.

Other productions include the British premieres of David Mamet's *The Woods*, with Peter Polycarpou, Robert's translation of Fermín Cabal's Ishoot! with Don Gilet, Raad Rawi and Danielle Tarento and *One God, One Farinelli!* with Richard O'Brien.

In June 2006 we presented the British premiere of *Ana in Love* by Paloma Pedrero, translated by Robert, with Maisie Dimbleby, Anne Firbank, Jessica Oyelowo, Isobel Pravda and Judith Scott.

Our other productions include *As You Like It* at Jermyn Street Theatre with Jessica Oyelowo and Michael Wildman, for which Robert wrote the music, and *The Investigation* by Peter Weiss. In opera, we have presented the London premiere of *The Medium*, performed by Jane Manning, and *The Lighthouse* (both by Sir Peter Maxwell Davies) and the world premiere of a commissioned work ...*I Sat Down and Wept*, with music by Chloe Dyn Tsoe and text adapted by Robert from Elisabeth Smart's novel.

Inside Intelligence has repeatedly shown a knack for launching remarkable artists on the path to recognition. These include Fermín Cabal, Vincent Ebrahim, Alfred Enoch, Don Gilet, Gerard McBurney, Jessica Oyelowo, David Oyelowo, Danielle Tarento, Michael Wildman, Joel Samuels and Aaron Swartz.

We are also proud to have worked with established artists including Colin Baker, Patsy Byrne, Raquel Cassidy, Oliver Ford Davies, Lisa Dillon, Athol Fugard, Julie Legrand, David Mamet, Jane Manning, Sir Peter Maxwell Davies, Richard O'Brien, Paloma Pedrero, Peter Polycarpou, Raad Rawi, Joely Richardson, Judith Scott and Josie Taylor.

# A NOTE ON TEJAS VERDES

This play is based on real events and real people. Tejas Verdes, which means Green Gables, was the name of a detention and torture centre operated by the Chilean Army in the months following the 1973 coup by General Augusto Pinochet against the world's first democratically elected Marxist government, headed by President Salvador Allende. The coup was followed by a notorious period of repression, torture, disappearance and extra-judicial killing. Some 3,000 people were "disappeared".

Tejas Verdes had previously been a sea-side resort for wealthy Chileans – the torture was carried out in what used to be the music room.

This coup was endorsed by the USA, Britain and other states. However, following the car-bomb assassination in Washington in 1976 of Orlando Letelier, the Foreign Minister in Allende's government, the USA changed their position. This assassination was planned by Manuel Contreras Sepúlveda, the Head of Chile's Secret Police, the DINA. Contreras was the commanding officer of Tejas Verdes in the period described in this play. In 1995, Contreras was arrested and imprisoned for this murder.

In 1990, Pinochet finally relinquished power, although he made himself Senator-for-life and passed laws giving him life-time immunity from prosecution. He remained head of the army until 1997. In 1998, while in London for medical treatment, Pinochet was arrested on an extradition warrant issued by the Spanish investigating judge Baltasar Garzón. Pinochet was detained in the UK for about thirteen months before he was allowed to return to Chile on medical grounds. However, a movement began in Chile to have him prosecuted there. Late in 2004, the Chilean Supreme Court ruled that he was fit to stand trial and lifted his immunity, paving the way for prosecution in his homeland. On 13 December 2004, General Pinochet was placed under house arrest in Chile on human rights charges.

By the time of his death on 10 December 2006, about 300 criminal charges were still pending against him in Chile for numerous human rights violations, tax evasion, and embezzlement during his 17-year rule and afterwards. Pinochet was accused of having corruptly amassed a wealth of US$28 million or more.

Freedom from Torture

Medical Foundation for the Care of Victims of Torture

## Freedom from Torture

Founded in 1985, Freedom from Torture (formerly the Medical Foundation for the Care of Victims of Torture) is a human rights organisation that exists to enable survivors of torture and organised violence to engage in a healing process to assert their own human dignity and worth. In the past 20 years we have helped some 40,000 men, women and children from more than 100 countries. Our concern for the health and well being of torture survivors and their families is directed towards providing medical and social care, practical assistance, and psychological and physical therapy. It is also our mission to raise public awareness about torture and its consequences.

We desperately need your support, so if you can help, please visit www.freedomfromtorture.org and make a donation.

CHILE
40 Years On

## Chile 40 Years On network

2013 marks the 40th anniversary of the Chilean coup d'état on 11th September 1973. The *Chile 40 Years On* network has been set up to commemorate the 40th anniversary of the Chilean human and social tragedy brought about by Pinochet's dictatorship.

"Thousands of people were tortured and killed, others 'disappeared' at the hands of the authorities and secret police, and more were illegally detained. Men, women and children were rounded up by the military and taken from their homes. Most were never seen alive by their families again. 1 million people were forced into exile.

The *Chile 40 Years On* network aims to link up and facilitate memorial events and initiatives to celebrate survival and life in different parts of the UK, so that there can be a critical mass of awareness of the significance of these events for Chile and the rest of the world.

## St John's Church

The Church of St John's the Evangelist was designed in 1816 by William Burn, one of the foremost architects of his day. The Church was opened for worship in March 1818. Daniel Sandford, who founded the congregation twenty-five years earlier, oversaw the construction of St John's Church. Sandford was also Bishop of Edinburgh from 1806 – 1830 and helped to unify the divided Scottish Episcopal Church.

In 1857-61 ten of the aisle windows of St John's were filled in with stained glass, the work of Ballantine and Allan of Edinburgh, two of the pioneers of the rediscovery of the technique of making stained glass.

In 1937 space below the Church was excavated and converted into rooms for various church activities. During the Second World War, they were used as rest rooms for service personnel in transit. Between 1940 and 1942 over 6000 service personnel slept there and were cared for by members of the congregation. For the remainder of the war they were used only during the day as rest rooms.

During 2001 the Church was completely repaired internally and re-decorated from its previous grey to the off-white and a new lighting system was installed. To this day St John's remains a thriving Scottish Episcopal church at the heart of Scotland's beautiful capital city well-known for its hard-hitting murals and its strong stance on social justice or fair trade.

## just Festival

just Festival started as the Festival of Spirituality and Peace in August 2001, organised by St John's Episcopal Church, Princes Street, Edinburgh as a contribution to the festival scene in Edinburgh in August. The intention was to affirm human creativity and the prophetic insight of much that goes on in the Edinburgh festivals – and to add a faith-based perspective on topical issues. The first programme was modest – a series of lunch-time conversations and evening hours for contemplation/meditation called Sacred Space.

One month later, in September 2001, events took place that moved the role of faith in our world to centre stage, for the worst of reasons. It is surely no coincidence that, since then, this festival has grown as we seek to comprehend the forces at work and how, in the shadow of violence, we can redouble our efforts to work for peace.

Therefore from 2005, working with Edinburgh Inter-Faith Association, Scottish Government, and others, the just Festival was established in its present form: interfaith, multi-genre, topical, and participative. It quickly established itself as an important part of the Edinburgh scene becoming a festival in its own right in 2007.

Today the festival works with over twelve faith and non-faith groups and over seventy charities and organisations to produce a varied and challenging programme. We are privileged to provide a platform for faith leaders, politicians, activists, academics, artists, and the general public to meet in open discussion and dialogue.

# TEJAS VERDES

First published in this translation in 2005 by Oberon Books Ltd
521 Caledonian Road, London N7 9RH
Tel: +44 (0) 20 7607 3637 / Fax: +44 (0) 20 7607 3629
e-mail: info@oberonbooks.com
www.oberonbooks.com

A catalogue record for this book is available from the British
Library.

ISBN: 978-1-84002-537-8

Cover image by Laura Andreu Sedeño
Photos of Tejas Verdes by Robert Shaw

*If anything is sacred, the human body is sacred*
Walt Whitman

*Most people underestimate their capacity to bear pain*
Training Manual of the CIA School of the Americas

*Indeed I tremble for my country when I reflect that God is just*
Thomas Jefferson

*I am writing these quick lines for my memoirs only three days
after the unspeakable events that took my great comrade, Salvador
Allende, to his death… Immediately after the aerial bombardment,
the tanks went into action, many tanks, fighting heroically against
a single man: the President of the Republic of Chile, Salvador
Allende, who was waiting for them in his office, with no other
company but his great heart, surrounded by smoke and flames.*
From the memoirs of Pablo Neruda, published in 1977

# Characters

THE DISAPPEARED

THE FRIEND

THE DOCTOR

THE GRAVEDIGGER

THE INFORMER

THE SPANISH LAWYER

THE SOUL IN TORMENT

# THE DISAPPEARED

The Bells of St Stephen's.

I've been listening to them ever since I was a little girl. They've been ringing in my ears every day and I wasn't even aware of them. I listened to them, but I couldn't hear them. This is much more common than you might think. You can listen and listen and listen and never hear a thing.

The screams of the condemned, the wailing of victims, the protests of the oppressed – we listen to them every day, they're everywhere. But we can't hear them.

We don't allow ourselves to hear. If we could, life would be unbearable.

For thousands of years, a woman would bear ten children and then watch eight of them die, or nine, or even... If three survived she was thought to be lucky. People would point at her: strong blood, powerful, good stock. Our mothers were women like this. They had the choice: weep for the dead or rejoice with the living. So they learned to nourish themselves with happiness.

Mankind wouldn't have survived any other way. We've learned to forget. We had to. Just think on that.

It's why you're probably not listening to my voice right now. Perhaps you can't, just as I wasn't listening to the bells of St Stephen's calling to God – but then God can't have been listening to them either.

I know you can hear me, though, so I've got to talk to you and to tell you this. My sister dreams about me. My mother prays every day. She kneels at one of the pews in St Stephen's and she prays and she prays and she prays. And like thick smoke, her words become entwined with the ringing of the bells and they rise up to heaven on Sunday and on Tuesday and on Thursday, asking God if I'm still alive. But God can only smile. He knows where I am. He knows the truth of this story. But he can't give her the answer, because if he did, she wouldn't be listening either.

I've lost count of the times I've screamed or thought or wept: Mummy, I'm in Tejas Verdes, Mummy, help me, I'm in Tejas Verdes. TEJAS VERDES!

My sister dreams about the fun we used to have in the garden. She dreams about our old lemon tree, about my graduation photo. My mother told me: you make me so happy, Colorina, and she patted my back gently, as if she was making sure I was still there. Then she went off to water the plants. That was all the reward I needed.

Bitch. Bitch. Who was your contact, bitch? Hit her harder. Where's the fucker hiding? Just tell us, you stupid cow. You're in shit already, don't make it any worse for yourself – the others have told us everything already. Don't play the martyr. We're running out of patience.

They'd put a hood over my head and I could hardly breathe for the heat. They threw me to the floor and ripped my clothes off. The buttons were popping off my blouse. I pressed my skirt between my thighs so they hit me unbelievably hard to get me to let go. Then they tied my feet together and hauled me up so I was hanging upside down from a pole by the knees, with my legs apart. I felt fingers going in me. Search the stupid bitch's cunt, that's where the bitches hide things. Go on, search her. They just laughed.

I felt a hot liquid running down over my breasts and my face.

They just laughed.

They began to whip me on my back, on my arms, on my ankles, then on the insides of my thighs, then on my stomach.

They just laughed.

Then they stuck the cables into my vagina, my anus and my mouth. They began putting electric shocks through me.

(*Long silence.*)

I don't know how much time passed, nor where they took me. They threw me into a cold room, where there were more people. I was still blindfolded and my hands were tied behind my back. My whole body ached, I was covered in burns, I ached until I could ache no more. I hunched my legs and felt the touch of another body. I huddled up next to it, it was such a joy to hear it breathing and to feel the warmth it gave off. The other body was trying to find me too. It pressed its feet against mine. Its hands touched me. We must have fallen asleep in that position, perhaps we lost consciousness.

I was woken by the bells ringing as if it were just another day, just another quiet, lazy day. That was when I knew I recognised those bells. I'm right by the house, Mummy, Sis, it's the bells of St Stephen's.

What a piece of luck.

Come on, fifty-four. Stand up. I wanted to obey, but my legs let me down. I fell flat on my face, I banged my head on the flagstones. Then they kicked me. I could feel their boots in my ribs, on my thighs, in my buttocks. They lifted me off the ground, grabbed me by the shoulders and took me away for more interrogation.

Do you want to listen to your mother screaming? If you don't talk, we'll fetch her in and kill her in front of you. Help me, God. Oh God, please help me. Shut up, Marxist bitch, God's not going to help you because you don't believe in him. We do. Stick the gun in her mouth, time to kill the stupid cow. No, I've got something better to stick in there. You're not bad looking, but you're a bit skinny. You need to put on a little weight.

They just laughed.

I was there for so many days. Who was your contact? Where did you meet? How did you stay in touch? Who are the members of the political committee? Where is the general secretary hiding? Where are the leaflets printed? Where do they get their money from? Where are the weapons? Your friend's singing like a canary, stupid bitch, now it's your turn. Let's try the electricity in her cunt again, maybe that'll teach her.

They lashed me to a stretcher made of metal. They hung me from a pole by my hands and feet. They put electricity through me. I was rotting all over. There was pus in my eyes and nose. My mouth had gone numb. I had no feeling in my vagina or in my extremities. My body was covered in cigarette burns. Talk, stupid cow, don't you realise the others have told us everything. Talk. We're running out of patience.

My sister dreams about me. My mother prays every day. Mummy, I'm in Tejas Verdes, help someone to get the message through...

Where are the guns, bitch?

My sister dreams about the fun we used to have in the garden. She dreams about our old lemon tree, about my graduation photo. My mother told me: you make me so happy, Colorina, and she patted me on the back, smiling. Then she went off to water the plants.

Everything's going to be all right. Everything's going to be all right. The doctor who examined my leg said everything would be all right. They know I don't know anything. My leg's infected, but there's no gangrene yet. They'll let me go and they'll be able to cure it. Everything's going to be all right.

Later I saw myself flying over some bit of sea, I don't know which, everything was a blueish green colour, deep and alive. I wanted to touch the earth, I felt so at peace and all around me there were endless flocks of doves flying in the same direction as me. A deafening noise shook me and I woke up with a start. I didn't know what time it was, only that I was freezing to death and although I was hugging Miguel's body, a terrible cold sensation was running up my spine.

# THE FRIEND

Colorina means goldfinch so they called her that because that's how she moved. You know, hopping about all over the place in some never-ending rush. But where would she be rushing in Tejas Verdes?

They took her out every day. She returned without saying a word, her apricot skin bristling with the terror, with the pain. She would drop on to the palliasse and I hugged her while she told me very softly what they said to her and what they did to her. Apparently some old soldier stayed with her after the torture and gave her legs a massage. Nothing more. Just a massage. And he would say to her: talk to us, girl, don't you realise the others have spilled it all already, don't make yourself a martyr. Talk to us, you silly girl, we're running out of patience. And this man would give her something every day: a bar of chocolate, a peach, an orange...

We shared the peach with a girl who slept beside us and was always crying. At least she couldn't cry if she was eating.

Of course they took her away, but nothing was ever found of her. Not a trace, not a leaf, not one breath, not a single hair, not even a flower to mark her passing, not one single breadcrumb to show the way, not a scream, not even a sigh.

I met her in Chillán, in the summer of 1970. We went there to do voluntary work to help with development in the area. I didn't care for her that much to begin with. I saw right away that she was from a rich family. Not that rich, perhaps, but she didn't go short of anything and when she went into the houses and saw the poverty there she opened her eyes very wide and just stood there in silence, staring.

One time I met her in the Plaza de las Armas, pretty drunk, waving a bottle of enguindado. At that time we were both finishing university. I'm going south, she told me. If only she had. They say in the south hardly anyone got killed.

But she stayed in Santiago. She fell in love with a guy who was with the Revolutionary Movement of the Left, a militant working as a social worker in the Health Train. His name was Miguel. I remember it perfectly because she used to make up love poems about him and kind of forget them again, because she didn't have a paper and pencil and there was no way to get them so the poems were always changing bit by bit, they never stayed the same. The only thing that never changed was that name – Miguel.

Maybe it's better that way. Poems lose something when they're written down. They lose their spontaneity, so she said. I laughed at her. But Colorina, how spontaneous can a sonnet be? That's how we killed time, waiting for them to come and kill us.

Oh yes, and we exchanged recipes. She taught me how to make cebiche and I went into endless detail about my grandmother's Spanish cakes: the sherry sponges, the Easter cake, the doughnuts, the "saint's bones".

One day they brought her in bleeding, one foot smashed to pulp: they'd shot her in the ankle. She said they'd done it by mistake and we shouldn't blame anyone: she'd suddenly felt a burning sensation and then heard the shot at very close quarters and they'd had it treated straightaway; a doctor came and bandaged up her foot, even gave her a sedative and they apologised to her...

They promised her she'd be out soon. I don't know if she believed them, but I suppose she did. You always need a hope to cling on to.

There was a crack in the courtyard wall and she would stare at the moon though the hole for hours and hours. She said she could see her father's eyes smiling at her. And she remembered the warmth from his knees when she was a girl and he used to read her a bedtime story. She would always ask him to read *Hansel and Gretel* and she cried when the birds ate the breadcrumbs and the children couldn't find their way back to their parents' house.

That's the story of our generation. We went into the woods and we never found our way out again. Our parents didn't understand us. They could only think about getting us out of the house. I would tell her these things to get her laughing but she took them seriously and her eyes filled up with tears.

My father did love me, she said. We'll probably meet again in heaven.

Probably, I said. Now I sometimes think they must be together already.

The last time I saw her, the day they took her away for good, a funny thing happened. Well, funny isn't the right word. She had a terrible fever, the wound had become infected and was hurting her dreadfully. That evening they informed her that she was going home to her folks and when they called her, Colorina took off her coat, which was very striking and made of very good leather, a present from my mother she said as if she were apologising to everyone, and she gave it to the girl who was with us and said: you keep it, Mónica, you'll need it, and she hugged her.

Then the door opened abruptly, several men came in, pointed at Mónica happily putting on the coat and dragged her out.

We didn't have time to react or to explain. After a few minutes they brought the girl back in crying, and then, finally, they took Colorina away.

And we never heard anything ever again: not a trace, not even a sigh, not one single breadcrumb to show the way.

# THE DOCTOR

So who are you going to believe? Are you saying that the word of a criminal carries the same weight as that of a servant of the fatherland?

What do you mean be quiet? Are you telling me to be quiet? I thought you wanted to hear my evidence. Isn't that why I've been ordered to come here?

So ask me. Ask away. I'll give you answers.

Torture.

Not that again. No, sir, there was no torture. Or not in my presence anyway. Punches, yes, and slaps and kicks and the odd beating, of course there were, I've told you that already. But torture is different, in my opinion. You should call things by their proper name.

Yes, I did recognise her. A young brunette, caucasian, with very pale skin and long, dark, straight hair. Narrow hips, pretty thin, short, small breasts, almost like a young girl's. And a particular way of walking, like a bird. They called her Colorina. I remember her very clearly. And I'll tell you something, my lord, she seemed like a splendid person to me. A fine girl, dignified and polite. Unfortunately, it seems she was seduced by a Marxist fellow student, a dangerous individual, a terrorist.

Raped? Then you know more than I do, my lord.

I stand by the report I drew up at the time. Bullet wound in one foot. Isn't that enough for you? Oh, yes, "the prisoner was savagely tortured and raped and then shot in the foot into the bargain". It makes a good story. The truth is it was an accident, as you can see for yourself if you take the trouble to read the prisoner's own statement, where she admitted of her own free will that it was an unfortunate incident and not deliberate.

People say many things, my lord, and obviously these Marxist militants are all under instructions to claim that they've always been the victims of the most appalling forms of torture. The things they describe are unbelievable, inhuman, spine-chilling. We women are the worst, I'm not ashamed to admit it. Because in these cases one is dealing with pathological hysteria.

Dominated by fear, which in reality covers a hidden desire, the hysteric imagines all manner of fantasies and assumes them to be real. This is a clinically proven phenomenon, my lord, and very well known since it was first described in Vienna by Sigmund Freud, when he realised that the hysterics who were attending his surgery were all claiming as with one voice that they had been raped by their fathers in the first years of their infancy. And remember that even Doctor Freud believed their tales to begin with. So as for this story about rape under torture,

I can assure you with all the weight of my twenty years' experience as a military doctor, it's a myth. A hysterical fantasy. That is my diagnosis.

OK, so let's suppose there might have been the odd case. There are psychopaths everywhere. It can happen. Let's suppose that carried away by an excess of zeal one individual goes too far, takes advantage, commits some atrocity. But that's not what this is about, not at all. This is about putting the entire Chilean Armed Forces on trial, exemplary soldiers who have sacrificed many years of their lives for the people, for the fatherland. Or have we already forgotten how the people of Chile begged us in the services to save their country?

I lived through the thousand days of terror and anarchy under Allende. I haven't heard about it at second hand, I saw it with my own eyes. We had to queue to buy even the most basic things, you couldn't even get toothpaste. Nothing was being made, the workers occupied the factories and didn't do any work; in the country, people occupied the farms and ate all the livestock. The idea was that we were all equal: all equally uneducated, weak and grasping and if someone worked and behaved decently they had to be stopped at all costs.

No, my lord, this whole fairy tale about the disappeared has been blown out of all proportion to damage General Pinochet and to demoralise the Armed Forces. The stories are quite implausible.

People are saying prisoners had thumbs or hands or even arms amputated, that they were castrated, that they were burned with blowtorches or welding arcs, that their chests were hacked open with machetes and molten glass poured in, acid sprayed over them, that their wounds were dusted with caustic soda, that red hot pokers were forced into their rectums, that women and children were raped, that parents were tortured in front of their children, girlfriends and wives in front of their husbands, that monks and nuns were murdered, that they were made to eat excrement, that they were infected with rabies, cholera, syphilis, that they were kept for whole days and nights without food or drink or sleep, that they were subjected to mock executions, that...

You want me to stop?

But do you really think these things are possible? That the army of a civilised country could behave in this way? Can't you see that it's some crude publicity stunt to discredit us?

You want me to stick to the facts? Well it's facts I'm referring to. There is the mandatory report, those are the facts, an unfortunate accident, willingly recognised as such by the victim. I treated her thoroughly. We became close. She was a good person. She only had one fault: she was stubborn. When she got an idea into her head, she wouldn't listen to reason...

I'm not saying that there was never violence. Of course there was, no one's denying it. Does anyone believe you can go up to a terrorist with a cup of coffee and some biscuits and say "excuse me, Mr Terrorist, please could you tell me who you're planning to kill, and where and when?"

My lord: you know that's not how you do it. You know it all too well. Your lordship must have convicted more than one person during these proceedings. So please don't let's be sanctimonious about this.

What's more, sometimes the innocent pay the price for the guilty. Like with this girl. My lord, I told her a thousand times to stop being silly, to have patience, to keep quiet. Did she pay me the slightest attention? Keep quiet, Colorina, that's the best thing to do, they've said they're going to let you go. Can't you see they've realised that you're no use to them? What they wanted was to catch your boyfriend. Well, now they've got him so they don't need you any more. They're going to let you go. What could be better than that? They're going to let you go!

If she'd listened to me, who knows, maybe she'd still be alive today.

Did I say she was killed? When did I say that?

My lord, I confine myself to endorsing the afore-mentioned report.

But I'll say one other thing: if you were so concerned with the rights of the prisoners, why didn't you report this at the time when it was actually happening? Or didn't you notice how the accused were appearing before you? Didn't you see the burns, the welts, the eyes full of blood?

No, no, no, I repeat that I do not say there was torture. It's you who keeps bringing up torture. I'm just saying… what I'm saying.

# THE GRAVEDIGGER

If anyone wants to know what this country is really like, they should come and watch me at work. I'd show them.

I'm the caretaker in one section of Santiago Public Cemetery. The caretaker, that's it. In other words, it's up to me to make sure the dead are left in peace.

As I've been saying, there's a very beautiful part where you find the mausoleums of the great saltpetre mining and ranching families. There's also the foreigners' section, the architects, the copper miners and the railway engineers. There are wide avenues of beautifully cultivated groves of trees flowering in spring and elegant gardens full of the most exotic flowers.

Mind you, it's like a ghost town. You never see anyone walking round there. A car might pass from time to time but that's it. Rich people don't care about their dead. They set them up nicely, for sure, but they seem to think their duty ends there.

You might get the odd loving couple sneaking in on warm days and doing their deeds in the most private areas. If I come across them I look the other way. I don't think they do any harm. The neighbours haven't complained up to now.

Then there's another, bigger, section, where the roads are laid out in squares, with lots of red plum trees. There you find these whitish yellow buildings with tiny alcoves adorned with flowers and little awnings to protect them from the hot weather. This is where the dead of the middle-class families are buried, comfortably set up for all eternity.

Then the roads start to lose their elegance, trees give way to bushes, the individual tombs disappear, along with the pews, the rubbish baskets and the public telephones. This all goes and only the columbariums are left surrounded by untended patches of ground.

And then finally, at the northernmost end of the cemetery are what we call the Areas, open patches of ground covered in weeds mostly, hiding the crosses with the names of those currently renting their plot. The people lying here don't own their graves so they're only allowed to be here for a limited period of time. When it's up their remains are moved to a common grave and someone else is buried in their place.

Actually sometimes, you know what the poor are like, if the gravediggers can see that a particular grave is well looked after, when their time is over, they take the bones out of the coffin and put them back in the same grave, underneath the new corpse. In this way the relatives of the old corpse can carry on bringing flowers on the anniversary. And, at the same time, one corpse can keep the other one company.

At the time of the coup, I was appointed to Area 29 which is where poor people were buried and also where unidentified bodies from the Forensic Institute were put: they would have a docket like NN and they were granted burial for six years because in those days you never knew if a court might come and claim them. It was all very quiet, no big ceremonies, everything done very quickly and surreptitiously. That's where I met my husband, Aurelio Morales, a thin man, dignified, hard-working, and in thirty years of marriage he never once failed to show me respect. How many could say the same?

I knew there weren't many.

I first noticed him when I saw him working in his free time on a kitchen garden which he'd planted just beside the retaining walls of the common graves. Clever man, I thought. No flies on him.

On the 11th of September, we were opening up that area, preparing the graves for the deceased who would be arriving that day. We were at this when we saw planes passing overhead and began to feel the artillery fire. Up till then we had only prepared graves and buried bodies but after the coup this changed, because then we had to go to the morgue, put the bodies in the coffins, load up the truck, take them to the cemetery, bury them, go back to the morgue and do the same thing day after day.

There were a lot of bodies, we couldn't cope with them all. We have a grey Ford truck and we used to make two or three journeys a day. Generally speaking they came two to a coffin, to begin with it was only one, but later they ran out of coffins and they had to put them in head to toe. Then they started appearing in canvas or in sackcloth that would tear and it looked as if the bodies were trying to escape. Some of them weren't even bodies, they were like... lumps of dough, nothing more than a sack of refuse. The legs and arms were rotting, which proved that they had been out in the hot weather for many days being gnawed by rodents from the river and such like. Others were also rotting, but chopped in pieces, hacked up, like... bullets sprayed from a machine gun.

We were living in a hut in a spot where there are now just alcoves, and they used to come and get us up in the night to go and pick up bodies. There were bodies everywhere, but we got most of them from the rivers, the waterways, wherever they were floating, in the Mapocho, the Saint Charles Canal, the La Punta Canal, that's where we got most of them, but also in the streets, they were just lying around everywhere.

What torment in those years.

We worked and we worked... Then at home my husband tried his hardest, but it didn't work, it just wouldn't go in. (*She laughs gently.*) Well no, I mean it did, but, I don't really know how to explain, there was nothing there, it just wouldn't happen.

The doctor said it was my ovaries. I think it was my head. Some of those corpses were kids, babies almost. To me they just seemed all shrivelled up, with that lost look in their eyes, like they were trying to see something in the distance, way beyond the tops of the mountains. And I thought: the dead are like foetuses reared in the belly of the earth.

And who wants to rear a dead body?

That girl we were talking about, I remember her well. That's how her parents were able to find her. They'd never have recognised her by her face: it was smashed to pulp, they'd crushed it or burned it, how should I know… But when her parents showed me the photo, I recognised her coat: a very expensive leather coat, that's for sure. The sad thing was it had been completely destroyed, the collar and the back were full of holes and it was covered in blood… She was very young, just a girl and she had long, dark, straight hair. She must have been very pretty…

When word got out that we were burying the murder victims there, because I don't know how people find these things out, but in the end everyone knew about it, Area 29 started crawling with people, going all round the graves gossiping, getting in the way, asking a lot of questions… We couldn't tell them anything because we were being watched the whole time by the DINA and if they saw you talking to anyone, they'd get you. I'm not joking. I'll tell you what they did to us.

My husband started to feel very sorry for that woman who came every day and sat on a pile of earth with a photo weeping and weeping and showing her photo to passers-by. The DINA left her alone because apparently she was the sister of a general who was a friend of the president. So my husband saw the photo and he said to me: that's the girl with the coat. He didn't have to say any more.

What torment in that coat.

So then Aurelio took pity on her and said to her: madam, come tomorrow at one o'clock, when the DINA go for their lunch, and I'll dig the girl up for you, but you'll have to bring me a warrant. And the woman suddenly stopped crying, looked at Aurelio and she must have believed him, because she got up, went away and came back the next day with a warrant, permission for exhumation and removal of the body, issued by the Ministry of Health. Makes you sick, doesn't it? If you've got the money, what's your problem? Anyone knows that.

Her children had brought along wreaths and a hearse, the whole bit, just like it was going to be a real funeral. Only the bottle of anis was missing. Since no one wanted to pick up the coffin, Aurelio and I got hold of it and put it into the hearse.

As they were leaving, she went over to my husband and said, What do I owe you? and Aurelio just answered: Respect, madam. The one thing you can't give us. And he bent down and picked up his hoe, then he beckoned to me and off we went.

Money's all that matters to people like that.

Two days later, while we were unloading the Ford, the men from the DINA came over to us and shoved Aurelio and me into their van.

They took us to a piece of empty ground and made us dig a grave three metres by two. I thought they were going to kill us both. I dug and dug and the only thing giving me strength was the thought that they hadn't taken my papers off me. My wallet was still in my pocket. Those sons of bitches never kill anyone without first taking their wallet.

Then the one giving the orders said we'd dug enough and told us to stand on the edge of the grave.

And I still had my wallet!

One of the bastards whacked my husband's legs from behind with the spade and Aurelio fell forward into the grave. They all started shovelling sand on top of him, while the leader pulled my hair, forcing me onto my knees, and said: you like to play at digging up the dirt, do you, bitch, well dig yourself out of this one...

They gave me back the spade, and I started digging up the sand like crazy. And straightaway I came upon the shape of Aurelio. I pulled up his head, he was still breathing, he hadn't lost consciousness and he removed the rest of the sand himself with his arms.

Then the DINA took us back to the cemetery. They gave my husband a bottle of pisco and Aurelio, who never drank, took a huge swig.

Pay very close attention, they said, the next time you dig someone up without telling us, you'll be taking their place. And there won't be anyone to dig you up.

I looked at Aurelio, his face and skin full of earth, and I thought: that's too much for me now. I've given birth to a corpse out of the bowels of the earth.

# THE INFORMER

Yes, it was me who grassed her up. If it hadn't been for me, she might still be alive today.

Or maybe not. It was a very long time ago.

It was her boyfriend they were after, Miguel Menéndez, a leading light in the university and my friend in the organisation. A real heavyweight.

In a way, it was me who brought them together. I'd met Colorina in Chillán, in the summer of 1970. We went there to do voluntary work to help with development in the area. I didn't care for her that much to begin with. I saw right away that she was from a rich family. Not that rich, perhaps, but she didn't go short of anything and when she went into houses and saw the poverty there, she opened her eyes very wide and just stood there in silence, staring.

Then I got to like her. She was a girl who made you like her, so fine, so noble, so... delicate. I never thought they'd go as far as killing her, I thought they'd get out of her pretty fast where Miguel was and then they'd let her go, but sometimes things go wrong, the unexpected happens... Some moron was playing with a gun and it went off. The wound developed complications, they had to put her in hospital...

I'm not saying this by way of apology. What have I got to apologise for? I'm simply telling the truth: I never thought they'd go as far as killing her. Others, yes. I grassed up others knowing they'd be killed. And that they'd do dreadful things to them first. The same things they'd done to me.

If you want to judge me, please do. That's not why I'm here.

I have nothing to be ashamed of. They tortured me and I gave in. It's that simple. And till the day I die, I'll carry the wound they gave me. You see, you betray everyone around you, your own people. Anyone you've loved, men you've been in love with, your friends, your family if you have to. And they know who to ask you about, because when you do give in, the more pain they cause you, the more you submit.

I open up my photo album and start turning the pages and there they all are, staring at me.

I was grassed up too. I was trying to rebuild the party in the capital, in Santiago, and one morning, when I had gone to a soda fountain to meet a contact, the man I was waiting for didn't come alone. When I saw them coming in, I remember thinking, it's happening. At last. It was such a relief.

I knew it had to happen one day.

Why didn't I leave? I could have done.

I could have.

But I didn't. I felt obliged to set an example.

Also, I never thought there could be such horror. How could I?

As soon as we arrived at Tejas Verdes, they undressed me, they groped me, they hung me up on a pole and spent the whole evening hitting me with their belt buckles until the ground was covered in blood. I was blindfolded, but being upside down for so long, the blindfold had slipped and I could see the tiled floor the colour of earth. And blood was flowing all over my body.

I don't know how I was able to bear it. I think I was so dazed that I just couldn't get the words out. Also, they didn't ask me anything specific. They just wanted to soften me up.

Then came the questions. During the second session, an intelligence officer appeared and things changed: they put cables in my vagina, my mouth, my ears and began to put bursts of electricity through me. I should have talked right there and then. If it was written that I was going to talk anyway, why didn't I just get on with it? But the truth is they'd only just got started with the cattle prod when I fainted, I had a few convulsions and lost consciousness.

So then, realising they weren't getting anywhere, they tried a different approach: they brought my son in, barely six years old, and stood him in front of me. They took me off to a toilet and Captain Ursustegui said: you'll need to look your best, you've got a visitor. I washed and dressed and for the first time, without the blindfold, I was able to look at myself in the mirror: When I saw myself I burst into tears, horrified by what they had done to me.

So when I entered the room, I could already hear the boy screaming. They'd tied his feet and his body to a chair and a man was holding down his hand.

This man was holding nutcrackers, and when I approached, he squeezed them shut and I heard my son's bones cracking.

Mummy, Mummy, tell them anything, tell them anything.

I screamed at them, you sons of bitches, you sons of bitches, and they hit him and broke two more of his fingers.

That's enough, I said, that's enough.

(*Pause.*)

My son now lives in Sweden with his father. We were already separated when all this happened, and I've never wanted to see him again.

No, I'm talking about his father. I've seen my son. We meet occasionally. He's grown up now and he has two children. We've only talked about this once.

When we met again after many years, he hugged me and said: it wasn't your fault. He kissed me and we've never talked about the subject again. What good would it do?

It's my duty to my conscience to make this statement before this committee, because I have a debt and I feel that if I can make a contribution – in some way – towards repairing the damage I may have done by collaborating with the DINA, I have an obligation to do so. I want to contribute to revealing the truth and to justice being done, within the context of reconciliation. For years, I have been experiencing a process of encounter with God and I have lived very deeply my commitment to the Christian faith. And I want, as far as it is within my power, to be faithful to the dictates of my conscience.

I know that Colorina has forgiven me. I know because at that time we were sharing the same prison and one day I told her. Hate me, Colorina, it was me. I took them to your house. And she hugged me and kissed me. And in spite of the blindfolds we always wore, I know she meant it. The hands never lie.

We hugged for a moment and when she could tell that I was calmer, she took a peach out of her bag and we shared it.

Some nights, through a crack in the courtyard wall, she spent hours and hours staring at the moon. She said she could see her father's eyes smiling at her. And she remembered the warmth from his knees when she was a girl and he used to read her a bedtime story. She would always ask him to read *Hansel and Gretel* and cried when the birds ate the breadcrumbs and the children couldn't find their way back to their parents' house.

And I said, that's the story of our generation. We went into the woods and we never found our way out again.

But I never thought they'd go as far as killing her.

Several months afterwards, I began collaborating in earnest with the DINA, along with other comrades who had also given in. Up to then they'd just brought me in from time to time to identify someone, but less and less as time went on: I'd betrayed everyone by then. One morning they led me to the office of an older man, fat, very friendly, who offered me coffee and cigarettes and asked me what I thought was going to happen with the rest of my life. I answered that I was trying not to think about it. So he said: Well it's time you did, my child, because we're going to have to do something with you. I didn't know this was General Manuel Contreras, the head of the DINA, a wretched criminal, the worst in Chile. But at this moment he seemed to me like a good person. He said he knew I had repented and that he had decided to take me on as an official of the DINA and he handed me a document with the conditions of work for me to read. He came back after a while and I asked him if I had a choice. His answer was: it's yes or yes. And he pulled out a wad of money. Take it and have dinner at the Reina. Officer Weinstern is waiting for you. He'll be your immediate boss.

It was a miracle. After a year in hell, they were setting me free!

That night I asked my boss about Colorina and found out what they had done to her. While they were torturing her, the Air Force, acting independently, had captured her boyfriend in a raid. Because the girl seemed reasonable and came from a good family, they thought they could make a deal with her and let her go. But no, the doctor who had treated her in the hospital had submitted a negative report: the poor girl had gone to her and asked her to draw up a medical report confirming the injuries caused her by the torture. And that was it, they decided to finish her off. She was handed over to the Air Force to complete her interrogation and a few days later she and her boyfriend were tossed into the sea from a helicopter.

And nothing more was heard of her. Not a trace, not even a sigh, not one single breadcrumb to show the way.

# THE SPANISH LAWYER

Ladies and gentlemen, I don't have a great deal of time, so I would ask you to keep your questions specific and relevant.

Yes. Where are you from? I thought so. Well, I'll answer your question as clearly as I can: in the first place I have to say that there is no legal case to answer. My client has not committed any offence recognised in law and without that no legal responsibility can exist. But more than that, the events it is intended to try him on are not within the jurisdiction of the Spanish courts and this has been acknowledged by eminent lawyers in this country and all over the world.

Yes, I do consider Mr González, our former Prime Minister, to be an eminent lawyer. His statements in support of my client have been most eloquent. There is no legal basis for trying a Head of State for alleged activities which occurred while he was in office.

Look, that's a question you will have to ask Mr Felipe González and I'm sure he'll be able to explain it to you. I confine myself to representing General Pinochet.

I think you are a bit confused about my client's character. It's easy to depict him as a cruel man who led his country into a bloodbath. The truth is that Mr Pinochet had no responsibility for the coup of 11 September. Just the opposite. Until 48 hours before the coup, and this has been documented in numerous witness statements, my client, who had been made Army Chief of Staff by Salvador Allende himself, was trying to halt the military operation, which had already been decided on by the Armed Services Committee, because of the chaotic situation the country was experiencing. Only right at the last moment and with the intention of preventing the even greater catastrophe of a split in the army, did he volunteer, against his real wishes, to assume the leadership of the coup.

You call that changing sides because you are a Marxist cretin. I call it exercising the greatest possible responsibility.

*(A mobile rings. The lawyer answers it.)*

Excuse me. I can't talk right now. I'm in a press conference. I'll call you in ten. Sorry. I'm expecting a very important call.

Look, I haven't got time to discuss this sort of rubbish, but I will say this: all political leaders, all of them in all countries, will always agree about one thing. You can't govern a country without occasionally taking difficult decisions. We have seen this everywhere, in Chile as in any other place. And here in Spain is no exception. Witness the intolerably cynical attitude of our own Mr Baltasár Garzón, this maverick, radical, so-called investigating judge, so beloved of the intelligentsia, who has had the temerity to have my client arrested in London despite the fact that he himself collaborated publicly with a Socialist government here in Spain which was at that very moment conducting its own dirty war against Basque terrorism.

And might even have won it if it hadn't been for meddling by all those people hiding under the mantle of an alleged democracy who were in fact simply protecting criminals.

The same people who now talk of human rights, while they laugh at the tragedy of the twin towers. They feel no sorrow. No they don't, and they can't deny it. Well not according to what they write in the papers.

Hypocrite yourself. Let's be clear about this. What would have happened if the alleged victims of Chile had seized power, which is what they were really after, and which is what the army prevented on the 11th of September?

No. No. I'm not talking about Bin Laden, or the Palestinians, I'm talking about the military coup on the 11th of September. In Chile. The dates just happen to coincide. I hope no one's going to start blaming my client for that too.

(*The mobile rings again. She checks the number and doesn't answer.*)

Well now you're changing the subject, because you don't have an answer to my question. Yes, what would have happened if the terrorists had seized power in Chile? Well I'll tell you: it wouldn't have been three thousand that disappeared, and it's not even three thousand, those figures need to be reviewed. I can tell you a story about one alleged disappeared who my chambers have located living the high life abroad in political asylum with another wife and other children... To put it in the Spanish way, he didn't disappear, he went out for some cigarettes...

But joking aside, no one knows how many would have disappeared, maybe fifty thousand. Or a million, like in Cambodia. Why not? You know that within days of the coup, the British ambassador wrote to Pinochet congratulating him on his victory and offering financial support. The British government gave him 2.2 million dollars, China 2 and a half million, America 3 million. They recognised the stabilising influence a man like Pinochet could provide.

It's easy to make firewood from a fallen tree. Attacking a soft target. Going for a poor, sick, tired old man, an illustrious soldier, when they're not even fit to lick his bootstraps. That's easy. What damage these so-called intellectuals do, undermining our institutions with their scathing criticisms, with their totally sterile attitude... They're the eternal pessimists, dreaming of an absurd fantasy world which will never be theirs. These so-called left-wing artists systematically represent great men who have defended western civilization as hateful, immoral, vulgar, ignorant tyrants. According to them Pinochet, Margaret Thatcher, Hassan II, even Felipe González himself are all unscrupulous riffraff, only interested in their own personal gain and all capable of committing the most wretched crimes: kidnapping, torture, murder even. But the reality is very different. I would like to read to you, if you will permit me, a very revealing paragraph written by my client, and published, if you want to check it, in his philosophical essay "Politics, Party Politics and Demagogy", published in Santiago de Chile in 1983.

This is what he says: "Nature shows us that order and a fundamental hierarchy are necessary. The planets follow a never changing order, which allows the perfect functioning of the structure of the Universe, which is the work of God. In other words, it is the creator who confronts us with a real world of stability, order and authority. Nobility only exists in relation to harmony, and to the extent that it sets limits within society." I repeat: nobility only exists in relation to harmony, and to the extent that it sets limits within society. "Those limits are called hierarchies."

This is the true voice of my client, who you are

branding a murderer. A thinking man, one who asks everyone to act responsibly. Is that what you do in your own profession? It is truly?

Don't make me laugh!

(*The mobile rings again.*)

Yes? Yes, hello, yes... Yes... Yes...

# THE SOUL IN TORMENT

The bells of St Stephen's.

No one knows how long they've been ringing, they were there when I came into this world and they're still there, mourning for so many things.

Today they're ringing for me. They're holding a funeral for my soul.

Because my mother prays for me every day. She kneels at one of the pews in St Stephen's and she prays and she prays and she prays. And today, which is the anniversary of my disappearance, she is praying even harder.

Poor Mummy.

When they took me away, my brothers and sisters didn't want her to know about it and they sent her on a trip to New York and Boston. The poor woman took advantage of the journey to take several copies of the White Paper which the dictatorship had produced. She never understood anything. And yet she is a good soul. I owe her so very much…

She brought me up in the love of God. And that love can only show itself by loving your neighbour.

My sister dreams about the fun we used to have in the garden. She dreams about our old lemon tree, about my graduation photo. My mother told me: you make me so happy, Colorina, and she patted my back gently, as if she was making sure I was still there. Then she went off to water the plants. That was all the reward I needed.

My father doesn't dream about anything. I feel his eyes watching me from the moon and his gaze comforting me while I walk hand in hand with Miguel. How I would love to be with him, to sit on his lap like I did when I was a little girl and he read me the book of fairy tales. But there's no resting for us yet.

My mother, on the other hand, is already at peace, she weeps and she is at peace, which are not at all incompatible. I would go as far as to say that weeping is what gives her the most peace. She has wept so much that now she watches listlessly as the drizzle falls on Santiago, as the windows steam up, as the street noise quietens down every day at nightfall. And then, before she goes to bed, she takes out the photo album and she weeps and she weeps and she weeps.

In a small urn she keeps some blackened remains. She thinks they are mine and that makes me happy. If she didn't believe she had found them, she would still be as desperate as so many women, so many mothers, searching for a body receding further and further into the distance.

I said so many. There are not so many.

Wounds heal. Everything is forgotten. Only the obscene presence of the tyrant keeps the resentment alive in people's souls. Soon the old man will depart this world and then a veil of oblivion will very quickly be drawn over all this. Merciful oblivion.

But even then, I, and Miguel, and so many others must continue roaming the valleys, the deserts, the southern icepack, right up to the highest peaks of the mountain range, because I'll still be compelled to talk to you and to tell you about this. Even if you can't hear my voice. Probably you're not listening to my voice. Perhaps you can't, just as I wasn't listening to the bells of St Stephen's calling to God. Just as God can't have been listening to them either.

We are not beggars. I am not here for you to cast your pity at me like breadcrumbs tossed to a cripple. Because I know you're listening to me, and my voice won't be silent, not yet.

My sister dreams about me. My mother prays every day. She kneels at one of the pews in St Stephen's and she prays and she prays and she prays. And like thick smoke, her words become entwined with the ringing of the bells and they rise up to heaven on Sunday and on Tuesday and on Thursday, grateful to God for having found me. But God can only smile. He knows where I am. He knows the truth of this story. But he can't tell my mother, and even if he did, she wouldn't be listening anyway.

But the bells toll and they toll and they toll. And they will go on ringing out for so many things in the world until one day, suddenly, they will stop. And men will look around them and they won't find birds or breadcrumbs or graves or peaches or walnuts or photos or the moon or laughter in the garden or embraces frozen in the depths of the sea. Then only the unbearable roar of silence will be heard. The time of truth will have arrived, the time when tyrants will weep tears of blood, ashamed before the magnitude of their crimes. And their eyes will seek ours, because only we can forgive them. Because on that day, at last, God will have awoken and in one final majestic peal, He will sound the hour of the Last Judgment.

WWW.OBERONBOOKS.COM